When Teens Self-Harm

also by these authors

Free from Panic
A Teen's Guide to Coping with Panic Attacks and Panic Symptoms
Monika Parkinson, Kerstin Thirlwall, and Lucy Willetts
Illustrated by Richy K. Chandler
ISBN 978 1 78775 818 6
eISBN 978 1 78775 819 3

Can I Tell You About Anxiety?
A Guide for Friends, Family and Professionals
Lucy Willetts and Polly Waite
Illustrated by Kaiyee Tay
ISBN 978 1 84905 527 7
eISBN 978 0 85700 967 8

of related interest

Can I Tell You About Self-Harm?
A Guide for Friends, Family and Professionals
Pooky Knightsmith
Illustrated by Elise Evans
Foreword by Jonathan Singer
ISBN 978 1 78592 428 6
eISBN 978 1 78450 796 1

My Intense Emotions Handbook
Manage Your Emotions and Connect Better with Others
Sue Knowles, Bridie Gallagher and Hannah Bromley
Illustrated by Emmeline Pidgen
ISBN 978 1 78775 382 2
eISBN 978 1 78775 383 9

Self-Harm and Eating Disorders in Schools
A Guide to Whole-School Strategies and Practical Support
Pooky Knightsmith
Foreword by Sarah Brennan
ISBN 978 1 84905 584 0
eISBN 978 1 78450 031 3

WHEN TEENS SELF-HARM

How Parents, Teachers and Professionals Can Provide Calm and Compassionate Support

Monika Parkinson,
Kerstin Thirlwall and Lucy Willetts

Jessica Kingsley Publishers
London and Philadelphia

First published in Great Britain in 2024 by Jessica Kingsley Publishers
An imprint of John Murray Press

1

Copyright © Monika Parkinson, Kerstin Thirlwall, and Lucy Willetts 2024

The right of Monika Parkinson, Kerstin Thirlwall, and Lucy Willetts to
be identified as the Author of the Work has been asserted by them in
accordance with the Copyright, Designs and Patents Act 1988.

Front cover image source: Envato Elements.

The information contained in this book is not intended to replace the services
of trained medical professionals or to be a substitute for medical advice. You
are advised to consult a doctor on any matters relating to your health, and in
particular on any matters that may require diagnosis or medical attention.

A CIP catalogue record for this title is available from the
British Library and the Library of Congress

ISBN 978 1 83997 596 7
eISBN 978 1 83997 597 4

Printed and bound by CPI Group (UK) Ltd, Croydon, CR0 4YY

Jessica Kingsley Publishers' policy is to use papers that are natural,
renewable and recyclable products and made from wood grown in
sustainable forests. The logging and manufacturing processes are expected
to conform to the environmental regulations of the country of origin.

Jessica Kingsley Publishers
Carmelite House
50 Victoria Embankment
London EC4Y 0DZ

www.jkp.com

John Murray Press
Part of Hodder & Stoughton Ltd
An Hachette Company

Contents

Part 4: Practical Strategies

Acknowledgements

Many thanks to all the young people and families who shared their personal experiences of self-harm with us and entrusted us to support them during difficult times. We dedicate this book to you.

We wish to thank Lara Fincken-Thorne for her valuable feedback on the manuscript.

● PART 1 ●

INTRODUCTION

CHAPTER 1

Introduction to Self-Harm in Young People

'I started cutting myself because I didn't know what else to do when I felt really alone and unhappy. The feelings would rush up and get so bad that I couldn't stand it any more. Cutting somehow made me feel relief, like I could feel something else. I didn't want to hurt myself, but it's the one thing that helped me to feel better and to be able to sleep.'

Parents, teachers or other professionals who support young people in various ways understandably become concerned when they find out a young person is self-harming. It's a natural reaction to want to immediately step in, help and 'make it stop'. You may have concerns that the self-harming behaviour could lead to health complications or become dangerous or even that it may lead to further harmful acts. You may also have deep concerns about the cause of this behaviour, why a young person would hurt themselves in the first place, and their general mental health and state of mind. These are common worries many adults experience in these situations.

We have worked with young people who self-harm and the adults around them for many years and, through our clinical experience and hundreds of conversations, we have developed a psychological understanding of these behaviours and helpful approaches for dealing with them. Here in this book, we are keen to share our knowledge with the adults who matter most in a young person's life.

We hope to educate you about self-harm in young people, bust a few myths, and hopefully reassure you and impart a sense of calm. We also aim to give you ideas about how to respond in helpful ways both to support yourselves and also to support the young people in your care.

Whether you are a parent, teacher or mental health professional, the best way to support teens who self-harm is to understand their emotional struggles and provide comfort and opportunity to help them regulate intense feelings.

We realize you may not have time to read a book from cover to cover, yet you may be seeking some information and tools to apply as soon as possible. With this in mind, we have presented the chapters as concisely as possible and have highlighted key points. At the end of each chapter, we present the main take-home messages and a set of reflective questions to invite you to think more widely about the information presented and how it applies to your situation.

Some young people who self-harm will need to access professional help and possibly therapy, and we make suggestions at the end of the book about how to seek further help. This book is not designed to replace the support required but rather to equip the adults in a young person's life to feel more confident about how to respond in calm and helpful ways. We will make suggestions about how to create an environment for the young person that supports their ability to live with and manage their emotions in healthy ways.

WHAT IS SELF-HARM?

Adults are sometimes baffled by self-harming behaviour and find it difficult to understand why a young person would resort to hurting themselves for sometimes no outwardly apparent reasons. If we stop for a moment and consider our own reactions in sometimes stressful situations, it may begin to make a little more sense. Whilst drinking alcohol, such as a couple of glasses of wine, is often seen as an acceptable social behaviour, it can sometimes become a way of managing our state of mind. For example, you might reach for a glass of wine after a stressful day at work or once the kids are in bed, or have a couple of pints of beer to feel more confident and 'happy' at a social gathering. Whilst this would not be considered self-harm by most, it is acknowledged that alcohol can be harmful to our health, especially when used regularly. It is also in some instances a way for us to manage our emotions. There may be other ways that adults manage their emotions, such as by online shopping, gambling, overeating, excessive use of social media, driving very fast or using recreational drugs. It could be argued that *any* behaviour which has negative consequences on the self could be considered a type of 'self-harm'.

When we think about the more typical ways that self-harm is viewed by the public, the health sector and the media, we think about acts that cause physical pain and harm to the individual's body, such as:

- Cutting of the skin
- Burning of the skin
- Head banging
- Pinching
- Biting
- Scratching
- Hair pulling

Whichever behaviour we are referring to, there is usually one common driver for that behaviour: to cope with and manage difficult or overwhelming feelings.

Self-harm is therefore a coping response. Most people would probably argue it's not the most helpful strategy, but it is a coping method nonetheless. The individual engaging in this behaviour is usually trying to find a way of tolerating emotions that feel overwhelming at the time and finding a way to carry on despite these very difficult feelings. What it usually *is not*, is a suicide attempt or wanting to end their life.

Many people in the public domain, and some professionals, equate self-harm with suicide attempts. In our experience these two behaviours are very different. Self-harm is usually about trying to find ways of coping and tolerating difficulties and is an indication of a young person's efforts to find ways to carry on despite these difficulties. Whilst there is some evidence that indicates self-harm and suicide can be linked for some individuals, clinical experience and information from young people shows us that we need to think about these two behaviours in separate ways.

We encourage you to always be curious about why a young person is engaging in any sort of self-harming behaviour. Obviously, if there are indicators, past or present, that the young person is thinking about ending their life, then this needs to be managed urgently, calmly and with the right help. We provide some suggestions at the back of this book of places and organizations that would be helpful to consult with when these concerns are present, and where to get more information. We always urge parents to raise these concerns with their GP in the first instance or the local emergency service if it feels more urgent. Equally, if your child is self-harming to the extent that you feel they need medical attention (e.g. for a cut or wound), we would also urge you to consult with your GP or practice nurse.

In the remainder of this book, we will not be referring to suicidal ideation or suicide attempts and we will be focusing solely on how to support young people who engage in self-harming behaviours.

> '*I kept the fact that I was scratching my legs a secret. I just knew that if I told my parents they would hit the roof and get really worried and stressed. I felt ashamed. I wished they could understand why I was doing it. I wished that if I told them they would stay calm and not freak out and just give me space.*'

In the following chapters we provide some information and reflections on reasons why some young people self-harm and give ideas about how best to respond. Whilst we give our professional views based on clinical experience, we aim to provide information from the young person's perspective where possible. We give suggestions about how to find 'Self-Calm' when supporting young people in these situations, and we outline practical ideas and strategies for building a safe environment and finding other, more helpful ways of experiencing and tolerating intense human emotions.

Key takeaways

- Self-harm is usually a response to difficult and/or intolerable feelings and is a way of coping with those.

- Adults can respond helpfully by staying calm and helping the young person to find other ways to manage and regulate their intense feelings.

Reflective questions

1. *What do you immediately think of when you think about a young person self-harming?*

2. *How would this make you respond?*

3. *Is this the only way of thinking about it or is there an alternative view?*

4. *Would that make you respond any differently?*

CHAPTER 2

Why Do Young People Self-Harm?

Self-harm is a puzzle not only to most parents and teachers we work with but also to other professionals. As you are reading this book, we suspect you too may be confused about why your child (or the child you teach or care for) is self-harming. You are not alone, even GPs are often stumped as to why a young person is doing this; one survey found that almost half of GPs did not understand why adolescents self-harm (CELLO and YoungMinds 2012). Teachers also reported feeling 'helpless' and unsure about what to say.

HOW COMMON IS SELF-HARM?

We know from our own experience and from research that self-harm is actually very common in young people. You probably also know this from experiences with your child, their friends, or children and young people that you teach or work with. Around 25 per cent of young people have self-harmed on one occasion (Wright *et al.* 2013), and a smaller number – probably around 15 per cent (Stallard *et al.* 2013) – self-harm more than once, often regularly. This is an enormous figure and confirms what we suspect – that self-harm is massively under-reported, and most young people do not seek help to manage it. One study found that less than a quarter of young people who self-harm actually ask their GP or health service for help (Ystgaard *et al.* 2009).

We also know that self-harming behaviours have been on the increase in recent years; for example, one study found that between 2011 and 2014 there was a 68 per cent increase in girls presenting to health services who had self-harmed (Morgan *et al.* 2017). Self-harming behaviour seems to be starting at a younger age as well; more pre-adolescent children are beginning to self-harm (Morgan *et al.* 2017); while a recent meta-analysis found a 21.9 per cent prevalence among pre-teen children (Geoffroy *et al.* 2022).

So, ultimately, we know that self-harm is common in young people, and we also know that it has been on the rise. It is also clear that lots of young people don't seek help. Your role as their parent, carer or teacher is therefore pretty crucial as you may be the only person that they tell. We will talk in later chapters about how you can respond if your child or a child you work with does tell you about this. We will also signpost you to other resources and services, as it might also be important to support and encourage the child to seek help from other professionals as well.

WHY ARE SOME YOUNG PEOPLE MORE LIKELY TO SELF-HARM THAN OTHERS?

This is a tricky question that is not easy to answer. There are quite a lot of different things that might mean a young person is more likely to self-harm.

To start with, let's look at mental health issues and see if there is any link. Many people assume that young people self-harm because they are depressed or have other mental health issues. This is not always the case. We see lots of young people who self-harm who don't experience depression or another mental health problem. What we do know though is that self-harm behaviour is more common in young people who experience high levels of anxiety or experience regular low mood (Ystgaard *et al.* 2009). All teenagers experience low moments or even low days from time to time, but young people who experience low mood a lot of the time are more likely to start to self-harm. We also know that teenagers who have struggled with mental health problems for a long time are at greater risk of self-harming.

Neurodivergent teens also seem to be at greater risk of self-harming. A report analysing factors associated with self-harm in 111,000 adolescents aged 11–17 years found that the incidence of self-harm presenting in hospital emergency departments was three times higher for boys with autism compared with neurotypical boys, and that there was a fourfold increase in self-harm amongst those with ADHD (Widnall *et al.* 2022). We know that people with autism often have more difficulty regulating their emotions and that daily life can be more challenging for neurodivergent teens – for example trying to regulate and manage sensory sensitivities, transitions and academic aspects of school life, being misunderstood or not accepted by neurotypical peers, teachers and family members. We also know that young people who are more impulsive, often acting without thinking, are more likely to self-harm. In the same way, young people who do lots of risky things (who are often more impulsive anyway) also self-harm more than young people who are risk-averse.

What happens in a child or young person's life and what goes on around them might also be important. So young people who have experienced really difficult childhoods, where they may have been subjected to emotional or physical abuse, are more likely to self-harm (Witt *et al.* 2021). Having a parent who struggles with their mental health may also put the young person at greater risk. If, as a parent, you are reading this book, and you do struggle with your own anxiety and low mood, it is important to remember that you are not the only one and that many other parents do also struggle. It is also important to remember that we don't really know why there is a link and that you are not to blame.

A child or young person's peer relationships may play a big part. We know, for example, that if a child has experienced bullying, they are more likely to self-harm (Plener *et al.* 2015). On the flip side, secure peers and strong school relationships seem to be associated with less self-harm (Stallard *et al.* 2013), so children who have good solid friendships may be less likely to engage in this sort of behaviour. However, we have worked with many young people who self-harm who have good friendships, so this is not always the case. Loneliness might also play a part. A large study that was conducted during the pandemic found that young people who felt lonely were definitely more likely to self-harm (Geulayov *et al.* 2022). The more intense the feelings of loneliness the more likely they were to self-harm.

UNDERSTANDING SELF-HARM

We have talked about how common self-harm is and what things mean a young person is more likely to self-harm. You may be wondering though, why do young people start to self-harm and why do many of them carry on?

Let's start to think about what sorts of things might lead a young person to self-harm. What triggers self-harm behaviour? What do they get from doing this? Does it make them feel better or maybe worse? Are they influenced by others? Are they just doing it for attention? The better understanding you as a parent, teacher or professional have about self-harm, the better placed you will be to support a child or young person. Not understanding why it is happening often leads to frustration, anxiety and sometimes anger. We know from our work with young people that these reactions, although they are understandable, don't help the young person, and almost always lead to them feeling worse.

Almost all young people we see talk about self-harm as a way of managing distressing or difficult emotions. These feelings could be anxiety, sadness, numbness, guilt, anger or shame. When these feelings become too big or too difficult to tolerate, young people self-harm as a way of coping with or as a way of trying to reduce these big feelings. If they are feeling numb, they use self-harm to actually feel something. We talked in Chapter 1 about how we, as adults, often manage stressful situations (or difficult feelings). We might grab a glass of wine, treat ourselves to a chocolate bar, or have a beer at a social gathering. Young people use self-harm in the same way.

'When I feel sad, I don't know what to do. I want to get rid of the feeling as I hate it, but nothing seems to help. So, I use a blade to cut myself. I feel a bit better after but then feel guilty for doing it as I know my mum will be cross with me.'

'I feel so numb sometimes I just want to feel something. So I punch the wall or hit my legs with anything I can find in the moment. It does help at the time, I feel a bit better, but later my hand and leg hurt, and I feel bad about it.'

Young people who self-harm sometimes express a sense of feeling isolated, particularly from peers, which can lead to the difficult feelings we have talked about. They may feel that they have no friends, or that even though they have friends, they don't really belong. They may feel that people judge them because of their mental health struggles, sexual orientation or for a different reason. They may simply feel they have no one they can turn to and so use self-harm as a strategy instead. As mentioned earlier in this chapter, we do also see many young people who have good friends but who also self-harm. Sometimes they don't feel they can talk to their friends about their feelings, or don't want to burden them, and are left to deal with those feelings.

> 'I don't know why I cut myself. I am really lucky; I have a great family and good friends, but I just feel alone a lot of the time. I can't talk to my friends about it, I don't think they would understand. The feeling gets so intense sometimes, I just need to release it by cutting. It does help but then I worry about my friend seeing my scars and asking me about them.'

Some young people have a difficult relationship with a parent, a brother or sister, boyfriend or girlfriend. For example, they may feel that their parents or teachers have too high expectations of them that they can never meet, and worry they will disappoint them. They may feel they are a burden to people, and so don't feel able to tell them they are struggling. Some young people feel that adults around them don't understand their struggles, and don't feel they can talk to them. All these things can lead to the young person feeling anxious, low or angry, and they may start to self-harm to try to reduce or stop these feelings. Some young people really struggle with spotting how they are feeling, and this can put them at extra risk of self-harming, as they are less likely to reach out for help or support.

Having a difficult relationship with another young person can also lead to bad or tricky feelings. If a young person is bullied, they are likely to feel anxiety, worthlessness or even shame, emotions that are really difficult to sit with, and so may self-harm to try and stop these. The strong and difficult emotions associated with a first romantic breakup can also be hard to navigate and sometimes lead to self-harm.

'I broke up with my boyfriend. I was so sad but also really angry as he treated me badly. Cutting was the only thing that seemed to help. I know it's not a good idea, but I didn't know what else to do.'

We also know school and academic difficulties can be a trigger for self-harm. Bad results in a test, poor exam results, negative feedback from a teacher can all lead to a young person feeling bad, whether it be anxious, low, worthless or something else. They then might use self-harm to manage these feelings. From our experience, the pressure of exams can be a precursor to self-harm in some young people.

'Everyone thinks I should do well in my schoolwork as I am bright. I hate the pressure. I worry I won't do as well as last time and everyone will be disappointed. The worry gets bigger, and I can't cope with it. Scratching myself just releases the anxiety a bit.'

What about the influence of friends and peers? Is a young person more likely to start to self-harm because they see their friends doing it? Parents often comment to us that a friend of their child self-harmed or someone they know at school did. Our experience is that young people may be influenced by peers who self-harm; it might make it seem like 'normal' or 'OK'. However, this is not necessarily a good reason to prevent your child spending time with a peer who self-harms; there are likely to be many influences. For example, young people also have access to a lot of information on social media, and we know that content about self-harm on websites and on social media forums is common. This may also reinforce the idea that it is a normal and acceptable thing to do. If the young person is struggling with difficult emotions, seeing, reading or hearing about what someone else has done to manage this, may well be enough for them to try it out themselves.

'Two of my friends self-harm. They scratch themselves and sometimes use a blade to cut their arms. I was feeling pretty low last week as I had a row with my dad, so I thought I would try it. It did make me feel a bit better. I am not sure if I will do it again though as I don't want scars on my arms.'

Finally, what about the role of attention-seeking in self-harm? We hear many parents and teachers ask if the young person is simply seeking attention by their behaviour. Although that may well be true, it is not necessarily as simple as it sounds. Some young people do acknowledge that they are trying to attract their parents' or other adults' attention by self-harming, but this is usually because they don't feel that they have another way of communicating their needs. By that, we mean that they feel they have tried talking to a trusted adult, but perhaps didn't feel listened to, or simply don't feel they can start that conversation. It might also be that they don't have the emotional language or understanding to express how they feel. Many neurodivergent young people, such as those with autism, find it particularly hard to verbalize their feelings to others. Beneath the need to gain attention, is almost always one or more of those same distressing emotions that we have talked about – anxiety, sadness, anger, worthlessness, guilt, shame... So, the young person is ultimately likely to be trying to communicate how they feel via this behaviour.

'I just want to be heard. No one seems to listen to me or gets it. Life is really tough, the teachers moan at me, my parents nag me. I just want them to see how hard it is. When I burn my hand, I do want them to notice, to think, God she must be in a bad place. But they just tell me off and say I am attention-seeking.'

Hopefully, you may now have a better idea about why some young people self-harm and it may be a bit less puzzling to you.

We hope this, alongside the suggestions we make in the following chapters, will help you to support your child, or a young person you are working with, who is self-harming.

Key takeaways

- Lots of teens self-harm, probably many more than we are aware of.

- Teens who self-harm may have mental health issues, but not always.

- Self-harm is usually a way to manage distressing feelings.

- These feelings can be caused by all sorts of things (e.g. relationship difficulties, feelings of isolation...).

Reflective questions

1. *What difficult feelings do you think your child (or the child you work with) might be having?*

2. *What might have led to these feelings?*

3. *Are those around them self-harming or have they read/seen things on social media?*

4. *Is your child (or the child you work with) trying to communicate something? If so, what might that be?*

◉ PART 2 ◉

HELPFUL RESPONDING

CHAPTER 3

Responding to a Young Person Who Self-Harms – the Initial Conversations

In this chapter we will outline the most helpful way to respond in those daunting moments when you first discover that a young person is self-harming. Often these moments come unplanned, and many adults report feeling uncertain about what to say and do. Although each scenario is unique, we know there are certain things that can help make these difficult conversations a little easier. More importantly, having spoken to many young people, we have good insight into what young people who self-harm want you to do. We are confident that there are universal things that help them during these conversations, as well as things that seem to make them feel worse. We have decided to remain focused on what works best.

As you will have read in the previous two chapters, self-harm is a way of managing difficult emotions. As such, it is important to remember that whatever the young person has going on in their lives, it is currently causing them a lot of intense and painful feelings – so much so that they are having difficulty managing these feelings. It may help to think of the young person as having a bucket full to the brim with distressing thoughts and emotions, and self-harm being the only way they know how to turn the tap and let some of those feelings out. Indeed, in Chapter 2, you read multiple examples of difficult experiences that negatively impact young people, exam pressures, turbulent friendships, breakups, family conflict. When responding to a young person who self-harms, the last thing you want to do is add to their 'distressing emotions' bucket.

As you read this chapter, we ask you to keep this at the forefront of your mind, so that as you apply the guidance below to your initial conversations with the young person, you remain firmly rooted in conveying compassion and awareness of their struggles. Most of all, we encourage you to remain calm.

TONE AND BODY LANGUAGE

Whether it is the first time you are hearing about the young person self-harming or you suspect or have been informed that there has been another episode of self-harm, the aim of your initial responsive conversations is to put the young person at ease, so that they feel comfortable and safe to open up to you, and also more willing to receive future support should it be needed. What you say will, of course, matter. However, the way you talk, and the position of your body will leave a more lasting impression.

Although it may seem a little contrived at first, we suggest that changing your seating position and body posture to be as relaxed as possible will help set up a more harmonious conversation. If the news of the self-harming behaviours (or recurrence of self-harm) comes as a shock, take a moment to pause and invite the young person to sit somewhere where you are both comfortable. Sometimes young people deliberately choose to share something they are worried about when the adult is busy or seemingly occupied. This is often a subconscious way of reducing the need for eye contact and avoiding confrontation. Softening your gaze or inviting you to sit side-by-side instead of opposite one another is, therefore, a relatively simple, yet sensitive and effective way of reducing anxiety levels and inviting cooperation.

In addition to posture, your tone of voice will also be a big giveaway as to whether or not you are on their side. Regardless of how you are actually feeling, make every effort to slow down your speech and use a warm tone. Most self-harming youngsters are highly anxious about how adults will react to their behaviour, and it is important to remember that even the most outwardly tough are, in fact, hurting inside and needing a deeply loving response.

'I'm not sure how Dad is going to react. He gets really upset and doesn't want this to be another thing he has to worry about. I don't want to make his life any more difficult. I really don't think he can handle this.'

'I think Mum will just think I'm attention-seeking. She's going to be really annoyed. I don't think I can handle another lecture from her.'

'She'll put on a brave face, but I know she'll be worried. I just don't want it to change anything. She'll probably think she did something wrong.'

'What if they lock me up or never let me do anything? They already hate all my friends. I tried to talk to them before, but everything just ends in an argument.'

KEEP THINGS FACTUAL

Learning that a young person is injuring themselves can be incredibly difficult. No matter the relationship you have (whether you are the teacher, parent or carer), almost all adults will carry a sense of responsibility towards the young person and all sorts of emotions are likely to arise; shock, confusion and fear are common. If you yourself are going through a turbulent time and/or struggle to regulate your emotions, then these feelings are even more likely to arise. If you recognize that this may be the case for you (and if you are the parent, it is almost certain that you will have a strong emotional reaction), then Chapter 4 will be particularly relevant. Optimizing your own mental health and learning ways to manage intense feelings plays an important role when it comes to being able to support a young person to cope when psychological difficulties arise.

In terms of your reactions, the less negative emotion you display, the better. Teens are particularly sensitive to other people's emotions, and if they read panic or shock in your response, it is likely to make them feel embarrassed, ashamed or even responsible for making you feel uncomfortable. They may even become agitated or angry. Remember, we don't want to add to that bucket, so whilst you are processing what you have been told or need to discuss with them something you have discovered, the best thing is to keep communication factual.

Repeat back to the young person what you have learnt about their self-harm behaviour in a calm and factual tone and check that you have understood things correctly.

Examples of calm and supportive fact checking:

- I found a blade in the bin today and thought I saw some scratches on your arm last week, have you been cutting yourself?
- Thank you for telling me, I just want to check that I've understood correctly. Yesterday you took your hair straight-

eners and pressed them on your leg deliberately, whilst they were on and still hot, is that right?

◉ So those marks on you, that's from your own teeth, and you bite yourself when you are alone in the toilets at school? Is that what you are showing me?

Taking the time to repeat back what the young person has told you helps to keep unhelpful emotional reactions to a minimum, and it also shows that you are really listening and interested in their experience. It is also important to have the correct information if you are later required to help the young person remain safe or need to share what you know with another adult.

ACCEPT YOUR PRIVILEGED POSITION AND BUILD A TRUSTING RELATIONSHIP

Self-harming is a very personal and private experience. Young people (and adults) do not easily share these experiences with others. Sometimes it is the case that an adult has discovered self-harm without the young person disclosing it, other times the young person has shown a high level of trust and courage in sharing what they do to themselves. Either way, having this information is a great privilege and it is important to convey that you understand that very few (if any) other people know this about them, and that you recognize that this puts you in a very privileged position.

The information you now have means that the young person has handed you their trust and hopes that you won't judge them badly.

Whilst it may feel wrong to accept the behaviour, when adults jump in too quickly to try and stop or prevent the young person from self-harming, they are inadvertently giving a message of disapproval, despite acting from a place of concern. This is counterproductive and often forces the young person to retreat to a place of secrecy. It can also fuel a sense of shame. Until the young person has a better way of coping with their circumstances, they may not feel able or ready to simply stop. On top of that, they know this is disappointing you.

'I know they're just doing what the doctors told them, but locking everything away makes me feel like I'm a prisoner. They don't trust me at all. I'm not even allowed to walk down to the shops any more or use my card. How does that help me feel better?'

'Teachers keep following me to the toilets and I'm not allowed a compass at school any more. It's embarrassing. They can't stop me anyway. I can just use a blade at home. I don't know why I did it, but I took a drawing pin from my classroom yesterday. I wasn't going to use it, but I just wanted to have it. Just in case. It felt sneaky, but also good to know they couldn't really stop me.'

It is not necessary or appropriate to condone self-harm, but rather than exerting control, which undermines the trust they placed in you, we strongly recommend that you support the young person by accepting their self-harm experiences and keeping your relationship positive. This is particularly beneficial if you are the parent. By becoming closer and more open in your communication, you may well be removing some of the stress that contributed to their bucket spilling over in the first place.

'Mum's a lot more understanding. She doesn't shout as much as she used to. When I'm feeling really rubbish, I just go and sit next to her, and I think she just sort of knows. She isn't asking me loads of questions. It's just nice knowing I'm not alone.'

Examples of taking a trusting and accepting approach:

- Thank you for sharing this with me. I know this isn't easy for you to talk about and I'm really proud to be someone that you can trust with this.
- I really want you to know that you are not alone and next time you feel like things have got on top of you, you can come and talk to me.
- If you ever hurt yourself again, please let me know. I want to be here for you.

EXPLORING CIRCUMSTANCES PATIENTLY

There is no need to rush to understand all the reasons why a young person has found it necessary to self-harm. Indeed, asking a young person outright why they self-harm is a sure way of getting a blank and defensive response. It is, however, highly likely that one or more things has created a significant level of stress for the young person, and the more they are able to open up about these things, the more likely it is that they will learn healthier ways of coping. Exploring these things can take time, however, and patience is important. We suggest you take a curious stance, but do not put the young person under any pressure to further share, especially if they seem reluctant to do so. The best thing to do is show an understanding that things must be tough for them at the moment and that you are available to listen as and when they want to share anything with you. Our experience is that once a young person knows this, they will come and tell you more another time.

Examples of being patient and taking a curious stance:

- It seems as though things have been really hard for you. If I had a magic wand, I would take all the pain away. I'm so sorry to hear you've been feeling like this. Together we can try and figure out a way to make life a little easier for you.

- There must be a lot going on for you right now. Is there anything else you want to share with me? If it all feels too much and you're not too sure how to put it into words right now, you can always write it down or come and tell me another time.

- Often when things happen to us or things aren't quite as we want them to be, everything becomes harder. I know that hurting yourself isn't what you want to do, but it just seems like it might help in the moment. If things are bothering you, there might be another way of managing it. I'm here if you want to talk about it.

Even in the best relationships, young people can struggle to open up entirely to people they know. After all, in your role as a teacher, carer or parent, these are not stand-alone conversations, and you and the young person may well have other necessary interactions that cannot allow for complete harmony and acceptance all the time. As parents ourselves, we are fully aware that remaining patient and waiting for your child to take the lead is not a long-term realistic expectation. Teachers too, have other children to consider and cannot always accommodate or achieve a stress-free environment in which to talk about things confidentially.

Our suggestion is not to put pressure on the young person to share further circumstances, but to maintain a relationship where they feel more able to open up to you.

If you feel there is more going on for the young person than they are able to share, you may want to discuss the possibility of seeing a mental health professional. It should be made clear to the young person that this person is not someone whose role is to 'fix' or stop them from self-harming but is someone that they can talk to about their experiences and learn more effective ways of coping. If you do pursue this further, we have included some resources at the back of this book and would encourage you to seek a professional who is skilled at supporting emotional regulation in young people.

Your role is not to be a therapist, but to be someone that the young person can go to if and when they feel they need extra support during turbulent times.

Key takeaways

- Have the conversation somewhere comfortable and keep a relaxed stance.

- Use a warm tone and remain calm.

- Keep things factual and check that you have understood.

- Convey empathy and show willingness to hear more about their struggles.

Reflective questions

1. *How would you feel having something deeply personal exposed?*

2. What emotions come up when you feel a sense of responsibility over something you cannot control?

3. What might stop you from responding in a calm and loving way? How can you try and overcome this?

4. How can you help the young person feel accepted and show support?

CHAPTER 4

Accepting and Regulating Your Own Emotions and Reactions

As mentioned in previous chapters, looking after and supporting a young person who is self-harming can be incredibly stressful, distressing, confusing, overwhelming and draining on your emotional and physical resources. This chapter focuses specifically on you: the carer and supporter. You may be tempted to think this is not so relevant in the face of what your young person is going through, but we are here to remind you that this is vitally important.

Focusing on yourself for a time, and finding ways of coping, has a double positive effect. First, it helps you to feel stronger and more grounded in order to support the young person in your care. It is a way of making sure your 'distress bucket' is not overflowing and you have ways of opening the tap to let some pressure out. Second, you have the opportunity to show and model to the young person that it is OK to feel distress and that there are ways to accept and regulate these feelings that don't involve self-harm. Modelling behaviour is very powerful. Humans naturally learn from each other simply through observation, especially young people from the adults around them. They may never admit to you that they are picking things up from you, but it's certain that your behaviours and reactions are setting strong examples and templates for the young people around you.

In the following paragraphs we set out some simple and practical ways that can help you to cope and recharge your batteries in times of stress. We also hope that some of these suggestions may help you to step back long enough to see things from a slightly different perspective, to see the bigger picture. This is particularly important when we are faced with difficult information and situations, because in a distressed state we can focus too much on the negatives and the details and not enough on the solutions and other possibilities. Some of these suggestions may appeal to you and some may work better than others for your particular situation. Pick out what feels useful to you and use them for a number of days and notice what impact they have.

YOUR BODY

Let's start with your physical wellbeing. We are all physical beings, and there's no denying the fact that if we don't look after our basic physical needs and health, this starts to make a real difference to how we feel. It may start as energy slumps or grogginess in the mornings or weight gain or loss. But after a while of not taking care of these basics we may begin to experience physical pain such as headaches, or catch lots of colds. The link between our physical and mental wellbeing is undisputed and therefore after a time our mood, anxiety levels and ability to handle stress may begin to be affected by not taking care of our physical needs.

Here are some basic questions to get you focused on your current physical state. Are you eating enough and the right things? Are you hydrated enough? Are you drinking too much alcohol or caffeine? Do you move your body and get enough physical activity? Are you sleeping enough? Are you spending time outdoors and getting enough natural light? Are you giving yourself moments of calm and deep slow breathing?

For one week, check the following self-care behaviours and do your best to make some positive tweaks if needed.

- Eat well and regularly. Blood sugar surges and slumps can play havoc with your mood, therefore not skipping meals and eating regular nutritious food will give you steady fuel throughout the day so you can handle things that come up with good physical energy. You know the stuff that's good for you, so no lectures here about what not to eat.
- Drink enough so that you are not thirsty and tired – dehydration often leads to a feeling of tiredness and sometimes hunger, and it can have an impact on mood.
- Check your caffeine and alcohol consumption. Alcohol is a known depressant, and too much caffeine can impair your sleep cycles. Could you make some tweaks here?
- Move your body every day. There are clear links between physical exercise and improved mood. This could be a walk, the gym, some yoga or Pilates stretches at home, dancing to favourite music, a jog, hopping on the exercise bike, going for a swim, doing some gardening or vigorous housework! Anything at all to get you moving for half an hour or more and to get your heart rate up a bit.
- Make sure you are getting enough quality sleep. Have some downtime in the evenings and perhaps try some light reading. Switching off all electronics will promote better sleep as will not eating too late. If you are struggling with sleep consider seeking some professional help.
- Get outside every day if possible. The outdoors has numerous positive effects on our wellbeing, both physical

and mental. Being in the fresh air, spending time around plants or trees, or near bodies of water or hills can feel incredibly calming and rejuvenating. If this is a bit of a challenge, either because of where you live or due to time restraints, do your best to connect with nature in some small way. Water a houseplant, spend time with pets, take a walk around the block and look at the clouds or stars. Every connection with nature in this way will help you to rest your mind a little and be able to recharge.

- Remind yourself regularly to breathe more slowly and more deeply. When we are in a state of stress or incredibly busy, or both, our breathing tends to become fast and shallow, and we tend to breathe into our upper chest. This sends messages to the rest of our body and brain that there is some sort of danger, and we can get caught up in unhelpful breathing and stress loops. Simply slowing our breathing can break this loop. Set yourself an alarm on your phone to remind you to stop and slow your breathing down. Breathe into your belly and into the back of your lungs and side of your body. Do this several times a day. If possible, set aside ten minutes in your day to just focus on your breathing. If you can develop a regular meditation practice in this way, it can have significant positive effects on your overall ability to stay calmer in more difficult situations.

If appropriate, talk to your young person (or to your whole class) about how you are taking care of yourself in order to feel better in general, and to improve your mental outlook. Take opportunities to model basic self-care behaviours.

YOUR MIND
Checking your thinking

Something we can easily get caught up in, particularly in times of stress, is stuck and rigid thinking. We know from psychological models that our thinking is very closely linked to how we feel and respond. Therefore, particular ways of thinking may be unhelpful to us because it may lead to us experiencing more distressing emotions and reacting in ways that may make us feel worse. Let us give you a couple of examples of stuck and rigid thinking to illustrate this:

- *Catastrophizing.* This refers to a type of thinking that makes us expect and think about the absolute worst outcomes in different situations, and it makes us think a lot about the future and all the terrible things that may happen. Not surprisingly, this makes our stress levels go through the roof and can make us react in really impulsive, panicky and sometimes unhelpful ways.
  - Thoughts: 'I can't believe Joanna is cutting her arms! This must mean she's terribly unhappy. What if she never stops? What about her life and her job prospects? No employer is going to want to hire her if they see such scars. She probably won't find a boyfriend who wants to be with her. This is ruining her life. She won't be able to have a normal life.' And so on...
  - Feelings: Stressed, anxious, overwhelmed, depressed, powerless, panicky, hopeless.
  - Responses: Keep telling Joanna she needs to stop this behaviour. Keep checking on her and asking her lots of questions. Keep searching the internet about self-harm. Cancel own appointments and social engagements in order to be home with Joanna all the time.

- *'All or nothing' thinking.* This is a close cousin of catastrophizing and leads us to only see a situation in one way, often missing lots of other relevant information. Again, this type of thinking, if we get stuck in it, can make us feel much worse and react in unhelpful ways.

  - Thoughts: 'Two students in my class are self-harming. I'm sure there's bound to be more. This is just terrible. I can't believe young people are all doing this and there's nothing we can do to stop them. Mental health is really such a problem and it's going to affect their grades. I feel completely useless as a teacher with all of this to deal with. What's the point?'

  - Feelings: Hopeless, useless, stressed, worried, low, unmotivated.

  - Responses: Avoid looking at information about mental health and self-harm, it's too depressing. Withdraw from other staff at school. Keep looking at students' arms to see if anyone else is self-harming. Drink a bit more wine in the evenings in order to 'de-stress' after work.

You may agree that in both of these examples above, stuck and rigid thinking can make the situation worse. When we look at it objectively, it's often easy to see that this type of thinking is not reflecting the whole situation or the whole truth of the matter. When we are stressed and caught up in it, it's often harder to get this 'bigger picture' perspective.

So, what can you do about it? First, stand back for just one moment and ask yourself whether you are caught up a little, or a lot, in stuck and rigid thinking. This moment to look at your thoughts will hopefully give you some idea of whether you need to allow for some different perspectives. Then try to think about the situation differently:

- What is another way of looking at this?
- What would your friend say to you about it?
- How much of what you are thinking is not the whole picture?
- What are all the other possibilities in this situation?
- Could it be that it may turn out very differently?
- How can you get more help with this?

Also, talking to someone about our problems can often help us to see things in slightly different ways. Finding a different perspective and breaking out of stuck and rigid thinking may help you to feel less overwhelmed with difficult emotions and may allow you to be able to respond in calmer and more confident ways.

What might you suggest to the two people in the examples above? What could they both think instead in these situations? What impact would this have on their emotions and actions?

Allowing our emotions to be

One of the things that you will be learning in this book is that young people who self-harm often have difficulty in tolerating their own distressing emotions. However, this is something that all humans at different points will encounter. From the tiny baby who is crying uncontrollably due to hunger, to the older person who is grieving the loss of their loved one, we all encounter different times when our emotions are very strong and make us feel as though we are engulfed by them. Some of us are fortunate to have acquired ways of tolerating these strong emotions through our life experiences and due to our personalities. Others of us may struggle a bit more with this.

As a first step, it's important to show kindness, understanding and compassion towards ourselves when this is happening. Allow yourself to have strong emotions and remind yourself that this is all part of the human condition. We are designed to experience strong emotions. Just like we would want to show this level of understanding towards the young person who is self-harming, we also need to be able to direct this towards ourselves. And what a wonderful thing this is to model to the young people who we spend time with.

Second, remind yourself that no matter how awful we may feel, or how strong the emotion is, it will not last for ever. It will probably not even last a whole day, and many strong emotions pass in a matter of hours or minutes. It is this big wave of emotions that we need to learn to 'ride', rather than trying to push it away, run away, distract ourselves or use other ways to hide from it. Being able to let the wave wash over us and be kind and gentle towards ourselves means that the next time this wave may be somewhat smaller. Pushing feelings away or 'cutting' ourselves off from them tends to make these feelings stronger and less likely to subside in time.

YOUR SPIRIT

Whilst discussing spirit may seem irrelevant to some readers, it is crucial to think about a deeper part of yourself in your quest for good self-care. This has nothing to do with religion or any particular beliefs that groups of individuals may hold about the world and our human existence. It is simply an invitation from us for you to think about what really 'brings you joy' and 'raises your spirit'. It is an opportunity to move away from all the 'must dos' and 'shoulds' and 'what would others think?' and move towards reflections on who you are and the things that nourish and uplift you.

Some people know straight away what brings them that little internal 'buzz' and makes them feel lighter, more energized, and more joyful. Others need to ponder on this for much longer before it starts to become more apparent. It's the stuff that immediately makes you smile a little (or a lot), and makes you feel lighter and brighter. It could be singing in a choir, or fly fishing on a river, or doing a little charcoal sketch, or spending time with a loved one, or playing in a team sport, or planting a little flower, or driving a sports car, or walking in the hills with a friend, or having that hot chocolate, or writing to someone, or running with the dog. These are just some examples, and the things that will feel important and energizing to you may be completely different. This is the beauty of going a little deeper into ourselves and discovering what makes us tick. We may uncover completely unique and personal things that have a special meaning just to us (and it might be crocheting!).

Take a moment to jot down a couple of things that always tend to lift you. Are you doing these things regularly or have they fallen off your to do list? Schedule them into your diary. Start small and slow but do it at least once a week. An hour or so per week spent on things that lift your spirit can be more energizing than you can imagine. Once again, it is an amazing thing to model to young people and it will no doubt fill you with more energy and positive emotion in order for you to be more available to support others.

Key takeaways

- Looking after your wellbeing in various ways is a must, especially when you are trying to support others and when facing stressful situations.

- Good quality self-care will mean you are better placed to support your child.

■ You will also be providing the young people around you with a great role-model.

Reflective questions

We have included many reflection questions throughout this chapter. Take a moment or two to jot down some of your own thoughts about the issues we have discussed.

1. *What one thing might you change this coming week that will help you to feel well and more energized?*

2. *In what ways do you model taking care of yourself to your teen? How can you do more of this?*

PART 3

PROVIDING NURTURING ENVIRONMENTS

CHAPTER 5

Providing a Safe Home

We hope that, if you have read the first two parts of this book, you are feeling more knowledgeable about self-harm and have a better understanding about why some teenagers hurt themselves and how to respond to their immediate needs. In summary, self-harm can be understood as an indicator that the teen is struggling to manage intense feelings. The sensation of physical pain can provide distraction from emotional pain, give them a sense of control over their bodies, or become a way of communicating that they are finding life overwhelming and difficult. As adults in a caring role, it is only natural to want to 'do something' in order to support a teen who self-harms. No doubt this is why you are reading this book. The rest of this book will, therefore, describe how adults can help to keep their teens 'safe' and less likely to hurt themselves when they are at home.

We have deliberately omitted specific strategies that prevent the young person from hurting themselves in this initial chapter and encourage you to address other ways in which you can help the teen to regulate their emotions in the first instance. Having listened to young people, we know that removing the opportunity to self-harm, before they are willing or ready to change this behaviour, creates more stress and negative feelings for them. If the teen you are supporting has expressed desire to reduce or eliminate self-harm then we have provided some information on how they can achieve this, with your help, in Chapter 7.

HOME MATTERS

Teenagers face a lot of pressures and demands – both school and leisure time can present challenges, with many teens feeling as though they need to mask who they are or try and fit in with others' expectations. Adolescence is hard for many and even more so for those who are more sensitive, are in the minority or feel different in some way.

> 'It feels like I'm the only one who finds it hard. I try and just go along with it, but then it gets to me, so I leave. I know it's bad and I should just be able to manage it. I just make up some excuse. I know I've let everyone down.'

> 'I try and hang back for as long as possible so no one will sit next to me. I don't want to talk to anyone. I just want to be on my own. I can't concentrate when people are talking. But then the teacher makes us sit in pairs and I can't remember anything. Then she goes around and asks us questions. Hardly ever asks me, but you still don't know if you're going to get picked on. I just want to get out of there.'

Facing these struggles on a daily basis can be exhausting and, just like adults, teens need access to an environment where they can switch off from stress.

A teen's home should be a place where they can rest and recharge, a secure haven where they can be themselves and feel safe and supported.

Unfortunately, the demands of homework, their instant availability via technology and continuous reminders of 'the world outside the home', make it very hard to relax. In some households, a busy schedule makes it nearly impossible to find time to unwind. Others can have the opposite problem – too much unstructured time. Despite seeming to relax and not doing very much, scrolling on phones or lying in bed can become unfulfilling. Worries and boredom can escalate, reducing opportunities to have more enriching and uplifting experiences.

'I usually just go to my room and start watching video clips. Sometimes I'm not even paying attention to it, but it's easy and at least no one is bothering me. I haven't really got anything else to do and it takes my mind off rubbish thoughts anyway.'

To help a teen who self-harms, provide them with a home life that feels 'lighter' and offers opportunity to move beyond negative feelings.

LIGHT-HEARTED ACTIVITY

Whilst chores and homework may seem a necessity, a teen that is overwhelmed is unlikely to be able to focus on these tasks. Instead of getting into battles over what should be done, adjust your expectations in the first instance and focus on supporting the young person to unwind. Even if they are dismissed or rejected, provide opportunities for light-hearted activity.

Support your teen to realize that distraction and enjoyment can be had safely at home.

Examples of 'light' activities:

- Playing board games
- Having a movie night
- Choosing a special dinner/recipe
- Setting up a home spa
- Making a family TikTok video
- Building a bonfire
- Selecting family photos to print
- Learning a magic trick
- Holding a quiz night
- Swapping clothes
- Starting a computer game challenge
- Having a beatbox contest
- Participating in a team sport (netball/basketball/football)
- Redecorating their room
- Learning a new skill together (unrelated to schoolwork!)
- Making some jewellery
- Constructing a display (adult Lego)
- Doing a craft activity (card making, knitting, painting)
- Baking
- Creating non-alcoholic cocktails or smoothies
- Dancing to their favourite songs
- Inviting a friend over
- Going on a dog walk
- Doing some 1:1 sport together (game of tennis, badminton, going for a run)

PRIVACY AND INVITING CONNECTION

Although you are likely to be concerned about what your teen is doing when you learn that they have self-harmed, it is vital that you continue to respect their privacy and convey a sense of trust. As discussed in Chapter 3, by your taking an understanding stance, a young person is much more likely to open up and come to you if and when they need support. Forcing a young person to be in your company is likely to be met with suspicion and will most likely be interpreted as evidence that you do not think them capable of coping.

Give your child space and privacy so they can believe in themselves whilst trying to develop more healthy ways of coping with emotions.

Some teens are less talkative and will be embarrassed to admit that they need to be around you. They may find it difficult to make the first move towards connection and perhaps don't quite know how to ask for help or what that would involve. We suggest that you simply be present and aim to share more space together. There is no need to engage in in-depth conversation, and, in many cases, focusing on something practical together can be more beneficial and comfortable for teens. Whilst giving an appropriate level of autonomy, ensure that your teen knows that you are available and that you like to spend time with them. Indeed, whilst adults may fondly recall the younger years and be secure in the bond they have with their child, it cannot be assumed that teens 'know' how much they are loved. They are unlikely to have the same strong and vivid recollections of their infant years, and teens are often surprised to learn that their parents would be willing to or would want to do more things with them.

'I get back from school and just hang out in my room. Mum gets in a bit later, so I don't really see her. She always lets me know when she's home, but by then I've normally eaten something and don't feel like coming down. Sometimes I'll join her in the kitchen, but if I've had

a bad day, I just keep to myself. I don't think she knows how tough things are. I know she's pretty tired.'

Since some self-harm behaviours are an attempt to communicate a longing to be 'seen' or to be 'heard' (often referred to as attention-seeking), increasing positive attention and spending quality time together may move towards addressing this need.

Whilst parental presence is no longer a physical necessity, and part of adolescence is separating from parents and forming new relationships, parental attachment and bonding experiences remain a crucial part of supporting healthy emotional development in older children.

Initially your teen may reject your company. Many young people are subconsciously 'testing' whether or not adult motives are genuine. If they confront you with this, we recommend that you simply state that you want them to know that you are there for them if they need you, and that you want to spend more time with them. Then back away from engaging in any further defensive reactions or pressure to do something with you.

Examples of inviting genuine connection:

- Let your teen know when you are home and invite them to spend time with you (make dinner together, watch a TV programme).
- Ask your teen if they would like to join you leaving the house for a bit (go for a walk together, take a drive, run an errand).
- Invite them to help you with an activity – not do it for you, but help you complete something (e.g. unload the dishwasher together, do some weeding together, take some things to the dump, decide what to give to a charity

shop, pick out something to cook, word a difficult email, time your workout, pump up the tyres together, help select a gift).

The more you can be together without lecturing or giving direction/advice, the safer your teen will feel in coming to you when they have difficulties and/or the urge to self-harm.

ACCEPTING YOUR TEEN

One of the most common statements we hear from teens accessing mental health support is, 'My parents don't understand.' Teens are highly sensitive to criticism and have highly tuned 'possible rejection' detectors. This is due to growth spurts occurring in particular regions in their brain (see Appendix A, 'Overview of the Teenage Brain'). From an evolutionary perspective, this may help them find the most accepting and secure social group for when they move away from the family home. For a while, this makes them more susceptible to misinterpreting others as being more negative towards them (better to be safe than sorry). If your teen is struggling to make friends, keeping up with social demands or feels 'different' to others, then they will have an even harder time as they may have fewer positive experiences to balance out the negative ones (perceived or otherwise).

Teens are often plagued by self-doubt and can easily feel judged by others. During this developmental stage, adults need to be thoughtful about how they communicate and be extra aware of their teen's feelings.

The most effective way of increasing your teen's self-esteem and helping them to manage their feelings is to validate their concerns. Many parents fall into the trap of disagreeing with the teen's perspective in order to try and make them feel better. It is hard to hear a teen talk negatively about themselves or jump to catastrophic conclusions before there is any evidence. When parents try to convince their teen to think differently, they risk making the young person feel misunderstood. We are yet to meet any teen (or adult) who can be told to think and feel differently. They may pretend to feel differently to please you or, if you have a more defensive teen, they may become angry and shut you out. Furthermore, if you appear not to be able to tolerate what they are feeling, then your teen may become even more overwhelmed when 'negative' feelings arise. (See the 'Fixing versus Validating examples' that follow.)

You may recall from Chapter 4 that modelling and showing your teen that it is normal to have intense and varied emotions is important. What message are we sending when we try to control and change how a young person feels and thinks about things?

No one likes to be 'fixed' or told what to think and do. Although you may not agree with your teen's perspective, showing understanding and validating their feelings will help them to realize it's OK to feel the way they do and that it need not be a big deal (i.e. they can move through the feeling without becoming further stuck).

FIXING VERSUS VALIDATING - EXAMPLES

SCENARIO 1

FIX RESPONSE:

Teen looks upset as they walk into the kitchen.

Parent: 'What's wrong?'

Teen: 'I forgot to do an assignment and it's too late to hand it in.'

Parent: 'Well that's not so bad. Just write your teacher an email and explain you haven't been feeling well.'

Teen thoughts: She just doesn't get it. I'm never allowed to feel sad. She asks, but doesn't really want to know. Just tell her what she wants to hear.

Teen: 'Yeah, OK.'

Teen goes upstairs on their own and starts to feel worse about their missed assignment.

The feeling of isolation adds to their initial upset and they struggle to cope with the rise of negative emotion.

VALIDATION RESPONSE:

Teen looks upset as they walk into the kitchen.

Parent: 'What's wrong?'

Teen: 'I forgot to do an assignment and it's too late to hand it in.'

Parent: 'Oh dear. That sounds difficult. When did you remember?'

Teen: 'Just now. I don't know how I forgot. Mr Brown's going to be really mad. I hate him!'

Parent: 'Oh, it's for History. No wonder you're feeling upset. I know you don't want to upset him. Is there anything you can do this evening?'

Teen thoughts: At least Mum's not upset and understands. I guess it doesn't really matter what Mr Brown thinks. I'll see what I can do tonight.

Teen goes upstairs and has been able to safely share and process their emotional experience with a calm and understanding parent. They are more able to tolerate the difficult emotion and think through how to handle the situation.

SCENARIO 2
FIX RESPONSE:
Teen runs upstairs, slams door and lies on their bed.

Parent enters room: 'You almost broke the door! What's wrong?'

Teen: 'Sam is such liar! She just told everyone that she saw me in town and now no one believes me. I can't believe she did that!'

Parent: 'OK, well it's not the end of the world. Who cares what Sam says? Your friends know you aren't lying.'

Teen: 'I closed the door for a reason – can you just go away!'

Parent: 'I'm not just going to go away, no. You can't just take things out on other people. Maybe Sam saw someone who looked like you? Just speak to her tomorrow. You mustn't always overreact.'

Teen: 'You don't get it! You never do! I'm not overreacting. No one will believe me and now I don't have any friends. Please go away!'

Parent: 'Fine. If you're not going to be reasonable, I can't help you.'

Teen thoughts: No one likes me. I must be doing something wrong. Sam is the one who lied, but everyone hates me. Not even my mum is on my side.

Teen sits alone in their room feeling rejected by everyone. They become increasingly upset and feel like there is no one to turn to. The fear of being alone and never having anyone becomes unbearable.

VALIDATION RESPONSE:
Teen runs upstairs, slams door and lies on their bed.

Parent enters room: 'You almost broke the door! What's wrong?'

Teen: 'Sam is such liar! She just told everyone that she saw me in town and now no one believes me. I can't believe she did that!'

Parent: 'OK, that makes sense. I'd rather you didn't slam the door, but I guess you must be pretty upset. Did your friends say they don't believe you?'

Teen: 'Not everyone has seen the message yet, but Chrissy has already asked me loads of questions!'

Parent: 'OK, so you don't know for sure, but Chrissy wants to know what happened.'

Teen: 'Yeah. And if people don't believe me then I won't have any friends left.'

Parent: 'Sounds like it's pretty important that they believe you. I'm sorry this happened. Is there anything I can do?'

Teen: 'No. I've just got to try and explain things and get everyone to see that Sam is a liar.'

Parent: 'I'll leave you to it, but if you want to talk more about it, I'll be downstairs. Sounds like you had a really awful afternoon.'

Teen thoughts: This feels really rubbish. I'm so upset with Sam and Chrissy for not believing me. Maybe I don't need my friends tonight anyway. I'll just go and hang out with Mum and face them tomorrow.

TAKE A NURTURING APPROACH

Being responsible for a teen can be a challenging and thankless task. Adolescence is a time of self-focus and inward gratification. This, coupled with the biological shift towards independence and capacity to recognize (and point out) adult shortcomings, can result in turbulent conversations and heightened levels of frustration. Nonetheless, beneath the drama and/or ill-judged decisions, teens are doing the best they can. They remain a long way off from reaching maturity (which we now know occurs around 23–25 years of age), and it is little wonder that some (in fact, as you read in Chapter 2, an ever increasingly high number) become overwhelmed and unable to safely manage stressors that arise.

There are countless books and parenting courses on how to raise confident, happy children. When it comes to teenagers, however, the more loving and nurturing aspects of parenting take a back seat and we are often asked how best to 'fix' or 'change' a teen's behaviour rather than focus on how best to nurture and support their development.

Let go of trying to control the outcome. Loving actions and acceptance of your teen support their self-belief and capacity to face and overcome challenges. When they feel like they are drowning, throw them a life raft that shows you care.

Examples of nurturing tokens:

- Bring them their favourite drink
- Make their bed
- Treat them to a surprise gift
- Give them a lift to school
- Cook their favourite meal
- Lend them something of yours

- Tidy their room
- Give them a voucher
- Suggest they invite a friend over for an evening (no adults)

Key takeaways

- Make home a place to unwind.

- Offer opportunity for connection.

- Accept your teen, validate their feelings and model emotional regulation.

- Show you care through actions.

Reflective questions

1. *What is the atmosphere like at home? Are there ways in which you can connect more with your teen?*

2. *How can you step away from arguments and let your teen express themselves (remember their opinion and perception is naturally going to change as they gain more experience – sometimes it takes a few years, sometimes a few hours!).*

3. *What activities are there for your teen to do at home?*

4. *How often is your teen left on their own at home? Is there a way to increase your physical presence at home?*

5. *How can you show your teen that you understand them (even if you don't agree with them)?*

6. *What small, thoughtful, thing could you do for them?*

CHAPTER 6

Reducing Distress at School

We hope that you now have a sense of how you can begin to provide a space where your teen can feel safe and supported at home, where they can rest and recharge from the pressures of life. What about those external pressures though? Can you change them or reduce them in any way? We will focus particularly on schools and teachers, as many of these pressures are felt most in the school environment, and an increasingly high number of teens are reporting emotional distress linked to their schooling experiences. We know that teachers can have a significant impact on the pupils they teach. What can you, as teachers, say and do in order to provide a safe learning environment for teens? How might you adapt the school environment to reduce distress and allow opportunity for healthy emotional regulation?

Let's begin by exploring more what pressures young people face and how you might be able to reduce those by 'changing the headlines', adapting what you say to and what you expect from teenagers during their school day. What messages do young people hear?

ACADEMIC PRESSURE

We see lots of young people who self-harm who talk about the pressure of work and of doing well at school and in exams. There seems to be an ever-increasing focus on grades and exams. This can be especially difficult if your teen struggles academically and worries about not meeting your expectations or doing less well than their peers. In contrast, it is also often a big concern for those young people who are high achievers. They often worry that you will be disappointed if they don't carry on achieving those high grades or drop a grade during their next test. Often unintentionally, adults around teenagers give the message that grades and exams are really important, and they need to do well to succeed in life. The legal requirement to stay on at school until adulthood has perhaps also reinforced this view. This can lead to feelings of worry, anxiety, sadness or guilt.

When day-to-day life is centred around 'working towards your future', many teens become despondent. Teens are naturally good at living in the moment and too much future thinking can be stressful and difficult for teens to grasp. The curiosity and ability to learn from making mistakes becomes lost, and, instead, schoolwork becomes a source of negative emotion.

Teens are told they must do well in school and exams – this can lead to feelings of anxiety, sadness and guilt.

For teenagers, we have also observed a drive or pressure to engage in a whole range of after-school or extracurricular activities. There are clearly benefits to this, in terms of health and fitness, or engaging and enjoyment in non-academic subjects. However, it also feels like an additional pressure, something all young people *should* be doing and stops the teen from being able to recharge and learn how to slow down and connect with family at home.

PRESSURE ABOUT THE FUTURE

Most young people we meet have some concerns or fears about the future. Again, this is often a result of the messages they hear from adults around them. Questions about what they are going to study when they have finished their GCSEs, what they will do when they leave school, what sort of job or career they would like.

It often feels like they should have their whole life mapped out when they may have no idea what they want to do.

This can lead to feelings of inadequacy or worthlessness, or just fear or worry about not knowing (when seemingly all their peers do).

PRESSURE TO CONFORM

This is a big one. Almost all teenagers want to 'fit in'. Not fitting in feels really uncomfortable for most young people and can lead to anxiety, low confidence and low mood. Adolescence is a time when young people are exploring and experimenting, trying to figure out who they are and what they want in their life. This doesn't sit well with needing to fit in, so they often feel conflicted.

Teens are trying to figure out who they are – being told to conform doesn't help.

Adults also often give strong messages about conforming: about the need to look a certain way, whether that be related to what a teen is wearing, how their hair is styled, whether they have body piercings; about what they watch online, what they view on social media, what music they listen to; about what they do with their friends, and so on. These messages add to the young person's already existing turmoil about themselves and their identity.

MENTAL HEALTH

It is ironic that young people are under a lot of pressure to have 'good mental health', even though that pressure can actually lead to more emotional struggles. 'Resilience' is a term that has become commonplace in schools and other environments – 'They need to be more resilient.' Resilience is often defined as a personal quality, a sense of 'toughness' or innate ability to recover quickly from difficulties. This is inaccurate and conveys a message that teenagers should be strong, robust and happy all the time.

Being told they need to be resilient often makes teens feel inadequate and not good enough.

We all feel sad some of the time, which is OK. Most of us get angry sometimes, feel unconfident, or worried. Experiencing a range of emotions is normal. However, teenagers often have an expectation that they should feel happy all the time, that they should be able to cope with everything, and it is likely that this belief originated from messages they have received. We need to change this message.

THE STATE OF THE WORLD

Young people are increasingly talking about world events and issues. This may be partly due to recent major events, such as the pandemic, and may also be related to the wealth of information that is readily accessible on social media. Many teenagers think a lot about climate change, and the impact on them and their lives. These are all pretty scary topics and by their nature are an additional stressor for teenagers. There is often an implicit message that young people should be doing something to help, to contribute, to try to resolve these issues. Although well intentioned, this adds another layer of perceived pressure and demand on already busy and stressful teenage lives.

We feel it is important to briefly mention the impact of the COVID-19 pandemic. Many parents, teachers and young people have talked to us about the significant impact the pandemic has had on them, their family and their lives. There is an emerging evidence base that confirms this, specifically that the pandemic has impacted massively on young people's mental health and wellbeing. It has affected their schooling, their grades, their friendships and their future. The toll this has taken on teenagers cannot be overstated, and young people continue to be given messages about its impact.

CHANGING THE HEADLINES

As we said earlier, adapting what we say to and what we expect from teenagers during their school day is really important. Our experience is that if we reduce some of the pressure young people feel, this can lead to some of those distressing feelings they experience also being reduced. So how can you, as parents, teachers and other carers, change the messages you give young people? What messages could you change and what messages could you convey instead?

Kindness and compassion

It is not only about what you say but how you say it. The tone of your voice and the words that you use when communicating with a young person will have a big impact.

Talk to young people in a kind and compassionate way – put yourself in their shoes.

Think about your own experiences as a teenager – how would you have liked your parents or teachers to talk to you? What tone of voice would you have appreciated? What words might have had the most impact? Was there an adult who did communicate with you in this way? What did you appreciate about the way they talked to you? Alternatively, think about how your closest friends speak to you, and support you. What is it about their approach that feels supportive?

Messages we can give about work and the future

Teachers are in the most powerful position when it comes to messages we convey about academic work and achievement, and we encourage you to think about how you might change these 'headlines'. Inevitably, you will want the children you teach to succeed and do well. The impact of the sense of achievement and pride that comes with academic success should not be under-estimated. However, it might be that we need a different message to the usual ones. The usual messages young people hear:

- You need to work hard.
- If you don't work hard, you won't pass your exams.
- You need to pass your exams to get a good job.
- If you want to be successful, you need good grades.
- You need to start thinking about your future plans.

If we are going to really promote adolescents' wellbeing, we need to start giving a different message.

What else could you say that would help reduce some of those distressing feelings they experience? What might be more important and more influential in promoting a teenager's well-being? Alternative messages we can provide:

- It's OK to not get everything done.
- We all have strengths and weaknesses; we are better at some things and worse at others.
- Being successful is about many more things than how you do academically.
- Try your best but please don't be hard on yourself if it doesn't go well.
- Maybe it's better to focus on the 'here and now' at the moment.

For some parents, it is really important that their children do well at school. You may be thinking that this sounds like you, or perhaps a friend or parent you know. Again, we ask you to reflect on the impact of these messages on a young person, and how this may lead to bad feelings.

By saying something different, you are not telling your teen not to work hard or study, but you are helping them to consider the bigger picture. Nurture and support your teen to accept whatever the outcome is.

Changing our messages about conforming

We all hold our own (often strong) views about what to wear, how to look, music, interests, relationships, and so on. As adults, we are guilty of conveying those messages to young people, who are likely to be struggling to figure out for themselves what they prefer and what they don't like. These messages can lead teenagers to feel isolated, unconfident and even worthless.

- You shouldn't wear all black, it looks really depressing.
- Why don't you go out to town like all your friends do?
- That music is awful.
- I know you say you really like Jade, but isn't it just a phase?
- That piercing looks really ugly, I don't see any other girls wearing one.

Hold back on expressing your views – this can be tough but is really important.

Holding back on expressing our own views can be very hard indeed. We are of course entitled to our views, but for teenagers, who are in a very important developmental phase of exploration, it is important that we hold back. We don't have to agree with our teen or the young person we teach, but we can listen with interest and curiosity.

- What do you like about that music?
- You are really creative with your clothes and make-up.
- I understand that you want to experiment with relationships.
- I don't really understand that show that you watch but maybe you can explain it to me.

Messages about mental health

We believe that it is important to convey the message that it is OK to be struggling, to feel sad or angry. This is not evidence that the young person is failing or is weak. We would recommend steering away from the term 'resilience' as it has come to imply a need to be robust and tough and to overcome any challenges. This does not feel kind or compassionate and places more pressure on young people. We could describe resilience as an ability to know your limits, set boundaries and advocate for your own needs so that you are better equipped to work through setbacks that may arise. Resilience is built through connection and opportunity to create a life that suits the young person's needs. Ultimately, it is the responsibility of adults around them to provide an environment that supports this.

Let your teen know it is OK to be struggling or to not be OK.

Here's a conversation between a teacher and a pupil who is struggling. The teacher is letting the teen know it is OK to not be OK.

'How are you getting on at the moment, you seem a bit down?'
'I don't know, I am just finding school really tough.'
'Sorry to hear that. Can you tell me a bit more?'
'I just feel really stressed and then I get demotivated and can't do any work.'
'That sounds tough.'
'I know I should be OK and just get on with it, there is nothing to be stressed about really, everyone says I am doing OK.'
'It's OK to not be OK. It's OK to be stressed even though you don't think there is a good enough reason.'
'Really? My parents just say you need to get on with it, toughen up a bit, and you have a good life.'
'It's not that easy though, is it? If you are struggling, you can't just get on with it.'
'No, I guess not but I think I should be coping better.'
'Well, you can only cope as you can. That's OK, that's good enough you know.'
'I didn't think you would say that. It really helps.'

How to change the headlines about the world around us

Messages about the world around us come from many sources. It is not just you as parents, or teachers who will influence what teenagers hear. As you know, the news, social media and other forums have a big impact too.

- We all need to act now to reverse climate change.
- Life is going to get harder with the rise in costs and shortages.
- Young people need to stand up and be counted, they are the future.

Although these messages are probably intended to be empowering for teenagers, they can also create more stress and pressure and lead teenagers to feel disillusioned and rather hopeless. What different messages could we all offer instead?

- Even with our best intentions, we can't fix everything.
- It is OK if life is a bit harder sometimes.
- Accepting what may happen rather than fighting it is also important.

CHANGING THE ENVIRONMENT

As well as changing the messages we give young people, it might be important to change their environment, the place they live, the place they learn. We talked in the last chapter about providing a more nurturing, supportive home environment. You could do the same in school.

School is the place young people spend most time in outside of the home and where they experience a lot of pressure and stress.

We acknowledge that this is something that as parents you may have limited influence over. Even teachers may be limited in terms of how much change they can personally make to the school environment. However, let us just think for a moment about what adaptations could be made and how that might have a big influence on the feelings and struggles that so often lead to self-harm.

Ideas to reduce pressure and stress at school:

- Reduce the number of GCSEs taken.
- Promote other options (e.g. non-exam options – apprenticeships).
- Have quiet, calm areas at school (particularly for neurodiverse teens).
- Find other ways of making the school environment less stimulating or challenging (smaller classes, shorter lessons...).
- Adapt a teen's school timetable (to allow more sleep, downtime, time away from stimulation and pressure).
- Consider other forms of education (online, non-mainstream, hybrid).

There has been a move towards promoting other qualifications (e.g. apprenticeships), but there still seems to be a preference for a traditional model of schooling with very few alternative options available. This may not suit all teens so are there any ways of adapting the school environment to better meet your teen's needs?

There is an evidence base that teenagers find it hard to settle to sleep at the times adults would consider the 'norm'. This has resulted in a population of sleep-deprived young people. For young people who are really struggling, finding a way of accessing education that allows a good night's sleep could be considered.

We would also recommend trying to arrange a meeting with your child's school to talk about what might be possible. Your teen is likely to have some ideas too so it will be important that they are part of this. Your child's teacher will be able to let you know what could be implemented in school and may have experience from other children they have worked with.

The education system does not suit all young people. In our view 'one size does not fit all'. It may be that for some teens, the school environment causes too much stress, and a different educational provision is required.

Supporting neurodivergent adolescents

It is often really difficult to 'see' whether or not a child is highly sensitive, neurodivergent or struggling with mental health. Masking is really common, particularly with neurodivergent teens; many teens are skilled at presenting as though they are fine in school. It is important to listen to parents and teens when they tell you this is not the case. Not all of these young people will have a diagnosis. We would suggest that schools can and should be flexible regardless. Do not assume a teen is fine.

Here are some ideas for adapting your school environment to provide a safe, and nurturing environment, particularly with neurodiversity in mind:

- Provide unrestricted access to a quiet area and give the teen the opportunity to regulate themselves when feeling overwhelmed.
- Take a preventative approach by allowing and encouraging 'tools' that soothe and help the teen to learn.
- Consider different seating options, table mascot, sensory item, headphones, snacks.
- Build a positive, safe and trusting relationship with the teen and their family. Aim to work as a team and prioritize emotional wellbeing by being flexible and offering choices around expectations and work tasks.
- Give the teen the opportunity to communicate daily their

level of discomfort and respect and validate their feelings. Take a genuinely curious stance.

Key takeaways

- Young people are exposed to many different stressors.

- Messages about their academic performance, their future, the world can also have an effect.

- Changing what we say to teenagers is important.

- Consider how to change their school environment.

Reflective questions

1. *What stressors does your child or do the young people you work with experience?*

2. *Do you notice yourself giving unhelpful messages sometimes?*

3. *How could you change what you say?*

4. *How could you or others change your child's environment to reduce some of those stressors?*

⊛ PART 4 ⊛

PRACTICAL
STRATEGIES

CHAPTER 7

Practical Strategies

In the last two chapters, we have talked about how those around young people (parents and teachers) can perhaps provide a more nurturing, less stressful environment for them. In doing so, we hope that a young person's self-harming behaviour may lessen as they experience reduced stress and pressure and learn to talk to and connect with those around them. In our experience, these interventions are most likely to lead to a reduction in self-harm. However, we are aware that parents and carers may also be keen for more immediate and direct 'strategies' to help young people in the moment to stop self-harming. Although we feel these strategies are ultimately less important, they do sometimes prove to be beneficial, and we have thus dedicated this chapter to more practical ways in which a young person can 'manage' their self-harming behaviour.

WHOSE RESPONSIBILITY IS IT?

As a parent or teacher, you may feel that you need to do something practical to stop your child, or the pupil in your care, from self-harming. Ultimately, it is important to consider that it is not your responsibility to stop a young person self-harming or indeed to ensure they have a range of alternative behaviours or 'strategies' to engage in. Regardless of what you do, a young person may well self-harm anyway. As discussed in earlier chapters, most if not all adults have probably self-harmed in some way (that extra glass of wine, or smoking a cigarette) at some time, and this is normal (albeit not terribly helpful) human behaviour.

As a teacher, you may be concerned that it is actually your job to keep children safe in your care. You will have safeguarding policies, that perhaps refer to self-harm, or you may have a specific policy about self-harm and how to manage this in your school. If this is the case, then it will be important to familiarize yourself with this and to follow it. Nevertheless, you will not be able to stop all children self-harming in your school, and ultimately it is not your responsibility to do so. You can however support the young person who is self-harming by using the ideas we outline in the earlier chapters and also throughout this chapter.

It is not your responsibility to 'fix' the self-harming behaviour.

Ultimately, the self-harm will only stop when the young person wants and is able to stop doing it. However, your child may have said to you, 'I want to stop but I don't know how.' In that case, you may want to make some suggestions to help your child or pupil to start to work towards doing so.

WHOSE AGENDA?

Using strategies to replace or to try and control urges to self-harm won't work unless your child wants to do so. So, it is important that you follow their agenda:

- Do they want to try and stop self-harming?
- Do they have any idea how they might go about this?
- What do they think might work or at least help reduce the urges?

⊚   Have they read about or heard about any things they can
    try (from friends, social media...)?

REDUCING OPPORTUNITY

Although we have said that it is not your responsibility to stop
your child self-harming and you need to be led by them, it may
be difficult to step back if you are worried about the frequency
or severity of their self-harming behaviour. It is ultimately your
job as a parent to keep your child safe and you may feel that by
standing by you are not doing enough.

**One of the best ways to limit self-harm in the moment is
to reduce the opportunity a young person has to self-harm.**

By that, we don't mean locking all the knives away and throwing
away all the razors in the bathroom. First, that is not practical;
and second, it may make the teen feel that they have no control.
However, it can be helpful to get a better understanding of what
they are using to self-harm and to come to an agreement to take
away temporarily the item they use to self-harm, or that the young
person agrees to put it somewhere that is less accessible to them.
This could be putting a sharp object in a high cupboard that would
be hard to reach or taking an eyebrow razor out of their bedroom
and storing it in yours – anything that reduces impulsive behaviour
and means an effort is required to self-harm when they have the
urge (i.e. that they do not have something 'to hand').

Urges to self-harm do pass and it is often the case that it will
have passed by the time the teen has had to search around or go
into a different room to find something. It is really important
that the young person is involved in this though and that you do
not just remove anything without discussion as they are likely to
simply find a different means of self-harming.

In a school setting, it may be collaboratively agreeing with the teen that they do not have any sharp items in their bag at school. It may be that you negotiate searching their bag each morning or asking them to hand over anything that they could use to cut themselves.

Talk to your teen about how they can make things less accessible. Try to be collaborative; don't tell them what to do.

ALTERNATIVE WAYS TO REGULATE EMOTIONS

Most strategies that are suggested to young people to manage self-harm are based on the idea we have discussed – that self-harm is a way of regulating strong negative emotions. So what other ways can young people use to manage those difficult emotions?

Distractions

Distracting themselves from strong emotions can be a sensible thing to do in the moment. It will be important at some point for the young person to try to understand those emotions a bit more and find ways of coping with them. However, in the moment, it may just be best to divert their attention to something else, as the strong emotion may lessen or pass quite quickly. What the young person decides to distract themselves with or use to tolerate the emotion in the moment will vary.

Help your teen find a way of diverting their attention away from their strong emotions in the moment.

Here are some different types of distractions:

- Physical
- Creative
- Constructive
- Comforting
- Fun
- Social

Physical activities can include anything that is physical. The key is that it is something the teenager thinks they could and would do in the moment and is practically possible. Here are some ideas:

- Going for a run
- Doing star jumps
- Tearing up paper
- Kicking a football
- Popping bubble wrap
- Shouting or screaming
- Dancing
- Using a 'fidget toy'

For some, having a physical outlet will be important. Others may feel doing something calming or comforting would work better. This could include:

- Stroking a pet or a soft blanket or cushion
- Listening to meditation or a calming app/audiobook
- Massaging their feet/hands
- Watching a favourite film, TV episode in bed
- Having a hot chocolate or a bath
- Doodling
- Listening to music

Some young people will seek out their friends when they have an urge to self-harm and find this is the best distraction of all. It can work well if they have good, trusted friends who are supportive and also can be a good distraction. Others may feel they need to be by themselves.

Different activities will work better for different young people. Try to explore with your teen what might suit them best.

Some teenagers find they are more distracted if they engage in something that is constructive or structured, where they have a particular task. Here are a few ideas:

- Sewing
- Knitting
- Baking
- Tidying their room
- Computer coding
- Painting their nails or doing their hair
- Colouring or drawing
- Making a video/YouTube clip

What is most important is that your teenager can imagine themselves trying out a particular activity. The aim is ultimately to allow the young person just to sit with the feeling and not to self-harm to manage or get rid of it. This is likely to be really hard, at least to start with. Even if it feels like a distraction doesn't help, it is worth persisting with as it may begin to help a bit more as time goes on.

Other types of activities that might also help the young person stick with the feeling without self-harming are what we call displacement activities and reinforcing messages.

Displacement activities

These are slightly different to distractions as their aim is to, at least partly, replicate the self-harming behaviours but in a less harmful way.

- Putting an ice cube against your skin
- Drawing on your arm in red pen
- Having a very cold shower
- Pinging an elastic band against your wrist
- Putting henna tattoos all over your body
- Drawing on previous scars

It may be that the young person does something that looks like self-harming behaviour or that replicates the pain they feel when they self-harm. So the teen could repeatedly ping an elastic band against their wrist or hold an ice cube to their arm. They could have a hot or very cold shower and exfoliate vigorously. Or they could draw red ink on their arm.

Displacement activities aim to replicate some aspect of the self-harming behaviour without actually causing any physical harm.

Grounding

Another activity that can help young people sit with tricky emotions is called 'grounding'. This really means trying to connect with your inner world (your thoughts, feelings and bodily sensations) and also with the outside world.

A very brief grounding exercise, which is often taught in schools these days, is the idea of noticing five things you can see, four things you can touch, three things you can hear, two things you can smell, and one thing you can taste. The aim is to connect with the outside world. Grounding can also involve noticing your inner thoughts, noticing how your body feels and what emotions you are experiencing. Here is a brief exercise:

1. Find a quiet and comfortable place to sit.
2. Now breathe in and out slowly three times.
3. Now look around you. Name five objects that you can see.
4. Close your eyes. Breathe in and out slowly three times.
5. Keep your eyes closed and listen carefully. Name five sounds that you can hear.
6. Keep your eyes closed. Breathe in and out slowly three times.
7. Keep your eyes closed and think about how your body feels. Name five things you can feel (e.g. your feet on the ground, your t-shirt on your shoulder).
8. Keep your eyes closed. Breathe in and out slowly three times.
9. When you feel ready, open your eyes.

There are many grounding resources available online as well and we have included some suggestions later in the book.

All these activities are easier to provide in the home setting. However, it may be that resources could also be made available at school. If a young person had an urge to self-harm at school, could they be permitted to go to a quiet room, perhaps with some of these resources available, and to choose whatever activity they felt might be most helpful to them in the moment?

Key takeaways

▨ The teen needs to want to stop self-harming first.

- You need to include them in any discussion about reducing opportunity.

- There is a whole range of distractions they can use (physical, comforting, creative...).

- Displacement activities help some teens.

- Grounding techniques can help your teen tolerate different emotions.

- Remember not all teens will want to try these things, and that's OK.

Reflective questions

1. *Does your teen want to stop self-harming?*

2. *How can you begin to talk with them about what to try?*

3. *What ideas might appeal to them?*

4. *How will you feel if they don't want to try?*

Overview

Self-harm can be a difficult topic to discuss and understand, particularly for those who are impacted on a personal level. If you chose to read this book because you are currently caring for a teenager who is self-harming or have come to know a young person who is hurting themselves, we understand how distressing it can be. Although you may feel a sense of urgency and drive to stop the self-harm behaviours immediately, we hope that this book has helped you to realize that this stress-driven approach can result in more harm than good.

As clinicians, we strive to take a panic-free, compassionate and calm approach towards teens who self-harm, and we aim to provide a safe and relaxed professional relationship where teens can share their emotional experiences, rather than becoming overwhelmed by them. Our intention in writing this book was to provide you with information, strategies and guidance on how you can do the same.

Whether you are a parent, teacher or mental health professional, the best way to support teens who self-harm is to understand their emotional struggles and provide comfort and opportunity to help them regulate intense feelings.

There is no single cause for self-harming behaviours and no single way to manage them, but we hope you can see that understanding the challenges that the person is having, and making adjustments in order for them to develop new ways of coping, is key to a positive outcome.

Whilst writing this book, we have held all the countless conversations we have had with teens in mind. We have shared with you how teens think and feel, and in doing so we hope you have a better understanding about the challenges and pressures teens face in modern life. The things that they encounter and are exposed to are completely different to what many of us lived through in our youth. Certain commonalities remain, however. Adolescence is a time of personal exploration, growth and learning (usually arising from mistakes made). What we know from the high rates of self-harm amongst teenagers is that many haven't yet mastered the necessary skills to cope with and regulate intense emotions. For all humans this is best achieved in an environment that is calm, safe and stable, and if teens knew how to cope better, they would.

Emotional regulation is best taught via modelling and providing an environment where connection and calm exceeds stress, tension and isolation.

Unfortunately, we are aware that many teens are not given the necessary opportunities to learn regulation, and through no fault of their own teens can become adults who continue to struggle to recognize and manage their reactions and responses to stress. Given the emotive experience of supporting a teen who is self-harming, it is very likely that those charged with the role of providing help will themselves be tested on their own ability to manage feelings. Invariably, your ability to do so will depend on your own circumstances and skills.

Taking time to regulate and equip yourself with healthy ways of coping is important for your own mental health, but also ensures that you can provide the most effective care for teens who are struggling.

Key things to hold in mind during conversations with teens who are upset:

- Acknowledge their struggles
- Take a non-judgemental stance
- Listen instead of offering advice
- Remain calm and empathetic
- Give the message that all feelings are OK

We strongly believe that providing teens with a home and school life that is nurturing and supportive is by far the best way to reduce the incidence of self-harm. We are also confident that the approaches covered in this book will support healthier emotional regulation and reduce the need for self-harm as a way of coping. And if a teen specially asks for your help in stopping self-harm behaviours, there are practical ways to prevent the likelihood of them engaging in these behaviours.

Things to explore with the teen as alternatives to self-harm behaviours:

- Removal of immediately available objects
- Distraction
- Displacement activities

All of these should be discussed in collaboration with the teen and be offered as a choice rather than imposed on them.

At the end of this Overview is a concise summary of the key points covered in this book so you can refer back to this if you need some guidance in the moment or want to refresh your memory at a later date. We recommend, however, that you read over each of the chapters and spend some time going through the questions raised if this is something you skipped or haven't had the time to do properly. This is the best way to increase your confidence in supporting a young person who self-harms and will ensure that the approach you take is personal to your circumstances and the individual needs of the teen you are supporting.

Lastly, for those of you wanting to think more deeply about the way you support teens who self-harm, below are some questions to guide and inform your future responses.

Final reflective questions

1. *How do I feel about teen self-harm?*

2. *In what way can I make a positive difference to teens who self-harm?*

3. *What knowledge or new insights do I have about teen self-harm?*

4. *How can I support teens to develop healthy ways of coping with emotions?*

5. *Is there anything I can do to ease stress and reduce pressure for teens that I know?*

6. *Is there anything I can do to ease stress and reduce pressure for myself?*

7. *What does a supportive, accepting and nurturing relationship involve?*

Concise summary of the key points:

- Self-harm is a common way of managing difficult emotions. It is not usually an indicator of suicidal intent and does not automatically require risk management. The level of harm and physical risk should be assessed on an individual basis.
- Young people who self-harm are experiencing difficult circumstances in their life that are resulting in intense and/ or frequent strong negative emotions (e.g. fear, shame, sadness, numbing).
- Try to gain some understanding of what is causing the painful emotions and be curious and open to what the young person shares. Is the young person communicating a need? Are they finding particular circumstances difficult?
- Ensure that you are able to model healthy emotional regulation. Take care of your own physical and mental health needs.
- Make home life as 'safe' as possible by reducing stressors and increasing opportunity for connection and rest. Support the young person to 're-set' their nervous system. Develop a positive and nurturing relationship.
- Be aware of individual differences and stressors in school. Provide a relaxed and curious learning environment and make accommodations when necessary.
- If the young person is willing, support them to engage in

less harmful strategies if needed. This will not change any underlying reasons for self-harm but may help to reduce impulsive acts or immediate physical injury and/or longer-term physical consequences of their self-harm behaviour (such as scarring, infection, bruising).

Appendix A: Overview of the Teenage Brain

- The teenage brain goes through a massive growth spurt, which begins in puberty. The parts to grow are the regions involved in impulsive and emotional reactions.
- The regions that support reflection and logical thinking have their growth spurt much later and lag behind until the brain reaches full maturity at approximately 25 years of age.
- Thoughts, decision and internal experiences are therefore heavily influenced by survival instincts and emotions. Teenagers are biologically more sensitive to things that may threaten their safety as they prepare for adulthood. For example: peer/family rejection; inability to attract a mate/partner; possible failure to achieve future demands/expectations; possible poor job prospects/financial stability.

Appendix B: Recommended Resources

ONLINE RESOURCES
Alumina

www.selfharm.co.uk

Free online self-harm support for 11–19s.

Calm Harm

www.calmharm.co.uk

Free app for young people to help manage self-harm.

Royal College of Psychiatrists

www.rcpsych.ac.uk

Information for young people, parents, and carers about young people's mental health. Includes information about symptom criteria for a range of mental health problems:

www.rcpsych.ac.uk/mental-health/parents-and-young-people

Guide for school staff:

> *www.rcpsych.ac.uk/docs/default-source/improving-care/nccmh/ suicide-prevention/wave-1-resources/young-people-who-self-harm-a-guide-for-school-staff.pdf?sfvrsn=e6ebf7ca_2*

YoungMinds

> *www.youngminds.org.uk*

UK's leading charity fighting for children and young people's mental health.

Support and information specifically for parents and carers on self-harm:

> *www.youngminds.org.uk/parent/parents-a-z-mental-health-guide/self-harm*

Mind

> *www.mind.org.uk*

Advice and support to empower anyone experiencing a mental health problem or those in supporting roles.

Charlie Waller Trust

Advice and support for parents or carers of self-harming children:

> *https://www.charliewaller.org/parents-and-carers*

The Compassionate Mind Foundation

> *www.compassionatemind.co.uk*

The Compassionate Mind Foundation promotes wellbeing through compassion.

British Association for Behavioural and Cognitive Therapies

www.babcp.com

Register of practising therapists in your area (accredited to provide cognitive behaviour therapy):

www.cbtregisteruk.com

www.babcp.com/CBTRegister/Search#/

British Psychological Society

BPS register of practitioner psychologists in your area:

www.bps.org.uk/find-psychologist

Health and Care Professions Council

Check if the psychologist or other health and care professional has the right qualifications and is registered:

www.hcpc-uk.org/check-the-register

FURTHER READING

Fitzpatrick, C. (2012) *A Short Introduction to Understanding and Supporting Children and Young People Who Self-Harm.* London: Jessica Kingsley Publishers.

Knightsmith, P. (2018) *Can I Tell You about Self-Harm?* London: Jessica Kingsley Publishers.

References

CELLO and YoungMinds (2012) *Talking Self-Harm*. London: Young-Minds. www.basw.co.uk/system/files/resources/basw_114035-6_0. pdf

Geoffroy, M-C., Bouchard, S., Per, M., Khoury, B. *et al.* (2022) 'Prevalence of suicidal ideation and self-harm behaviours in children aged 12 years and younger: A systematic review and meta-analysis.' *The Lancet Psychiatry* 9, 9, 703–714. doi:10.1016/S2215-0366(22)00193-6

Geulayov, G., Mansfield, K., Jindra, C., Hawton, K. and Fazel, M. (2022) 'Loneliness and self-harm in adolescents during the first national COVID-19 lockdown: Results from a survey of 10,000 secondary school pupils in England.' *Current Psychology* [Advance online publication]. doi:10.1007/s12144-022-03651-5

Morgan, C., Webb, R., Carr, M., Kontopantelis, E. *et al.* (2017) 'Incidence, clinical management, and mortality risk following self-harm among children and adolescents: Cohort study in primary care.' *BMJ 359*, j4351. doi:10.1136/bmj.j4351

Plener, P., Schumacher, T., Munz, L. and Groschwitz, R. (2015) 'The longitudinal course of non-suicidal self-injury and deliberate self-harm: A systematic review of the literature.' *Borderline Personality Disorder and Emotional Dysregulation 2*, 2. doi:10.1186/s40479-014-0024-3

Stallard, P., Spears, M., Montgomery, A., Phillips, R. and Sayal, K. (2013) 'Self-harm in young adolescents (12–16 years): Onset and short-term continuation in a community sample.' *BMC Psychiatry 13*, 328. doi:10.1186/1471-244X-13-328

Widnall, E., Adams, E., Plackett, R. Winstone L. *et al.* (2022) 'Adolescent experiences of the COVID-19 pandemic and school closures and implications for mental health, peer relationships and learning:

A qualitative study in South-West England.' *International Journal of Environmental Research and Public Health 19*, 12. doi:10.3390/ijerph19127163

Witt, K., Hetrick, S., Rajaram, G., Hazell, P. *et al.* (2021) 'Interventions for self-harm in children and adolescents.' *Cochrane Database Systematic Reviews 3*, doi:10.1002/14651858.CD013667.pub2

Wright, B., Hooke, N., Neupert, S., Nyein, C. and Ker, S. (2013) 'Young people who cut themselves: Can understanding the reasons guide the treatment?' *Advances in Psychiatric Treatment 19*, 446–456.

Ystgaard, M., Arensman, E., Hawton, K., Madge, N. *et al.* (2009) 'Deliberate self-harm in adolescents: Comparison between those who receive help following self-harm and those who do not.' *Journal of Adolescence 32*, 875–891.